Asia and the Pacific

GEOFFREY HAWTHORN

PHŒNIX

A PHOENIX PAPERBACK

First published in Great Britain in 1998 by
Phoenix, a division of the Orion Publishing Group Ltd
Orion House
5 Upper Saint Martin's Lane
London, WC2H 9EA

A CIP catalogue record for this book is available
from the British Library.

ISBN 0 297 81922 4

Typeset by SetSystems Ltd, Saffron Walden
Set in 9/14 Stone Serif
Printed in Great Britain by
Clays Ltd, St Ives plc

Asia and the Pacific

I

Religion is dead, nature has been mastered, and the possible contents of life are known. There is nothing left to oppose, nothing left to think. Politics is at an end and administration rules. All that remains is to live lives of pure form. That was the Hegelian philosopher Alexandre Kojève's picture in the 1960s of the end of history, and he thought he saw it in Japan. Many now celebrate its coming in Singapore. The New Labour Prime Minister in Britain, the Conservative former chair of the House of Commons Committee on Foreign Affairs and Kim Jong-U, the director of a free economic zone in North Korea, together, less surprisingly, with Tung Chee-hwa, chief executive of the new Hong Kong, and an American consultant on 'good governance' for the Asian Development Bank, have each in their different ways remarked on what Kim described as the combination in that prosperous and eerily peaceful state of 'great freedom in business activities' and 'good order, discipline and observation of the laws'.

Kojève cast his conceit in the universalizing, historicist idiom of the West. This is not an idiom with which those in east Asia have been at ease. Nothing in their intellectual traditions inclines them to think of irreversible progress to an end for all mankind. This is not to say that they have not had their own presumptions. China became used to thinking of itself as eternally enlightened. Writers in seventeenth-

and eighteenth-century Japan delighted in the ancient sages. Even into the late nineteenth century, the court of the 'hermit kingdom' of Korea saw no reason to deal with outsiders. There was enlightenment in Asia, but it lay outside our time.

It was the European powers and the United States that brought it in. They arrived in the nineteenth century convinced that their Enlightenment showed Asia's not to be. (They also brought Christian missions.) As so often in such encounters, the humiliated came to admire the agents of their humiliation. The Meiji reformers in Japan in the 1870s and 1880s were the first of many in east Asia to use the West to define their own culture and imagine how it might advance. (Some contemporaries even asked whether the Confucian injunctions to be humane and fair were not more observed in America than in Japan itself.) To the seven elder statesmen, the *genro*, who were constructing a new Japan, the West also presented a practical future. Critical intellectuals were excited. Liberals were eventually silenced in China in the civil war that followed the collapse of the Ch'ing regime in 1911 and in Japan in the reaction in that country at the end of the 1920s. But various sorts of socialist and radical nationalist were to flourish in China and in Japan's colonies in north-east Asia and those of the European powers in the south-east. In the post-war years, reforming socialists had an influence in Japan, and revolutionaries came to power in North Korea, China, Laos, Cambodia and Vietnam; revolutionaries succeeded in Taiwan too, although with a different ideology, and by a different route. Now, however, liberalism has been all but confined to constitutions, socialism survives only in a few empty rhetorics of state, nationalism is *raison d'état*, and practical success appears to be all but assured. It was the West that caused east Asians to think of themselves in history. Some now believe that history might be theirs.

II

The servants of the more openly censorious states, like Kim Jong-U in North Korea and Tung Chee-hwa in the new Hong Kong, express their confidence with prudent practicality. The leaders are more forthright. Lee Kuan Yew, the founder and at the time of writing First Minister still of the state of Singapore, and Mohammad Mahatir, the Prime Minister of Malaysia, have been strident advocates of 'Asian values'. The popular intellectuals offer a gloss. Americans, the Japanese Yasusuke Murakami has said, think in a 'transcendental' fashion, and are principled, rigid and intolerant. East Asians, by contrast, operate in a 'hermeneutic' mode. They are liberals of a more humane, 'polymorphous' sort, sensitive to context. According to a collection of academics, journalists, executives and civil servants who met to think about Japan's strategy in 1994, it is this east Asian 'system', with its emphasis on 'conciliation and compromise', that is the 'new universal'.

Few would put it so strongly. But students of east Asia agree that there is something that sets it apart. They often suggest that this lies in belief. In the Chinese societies, it has commonly been called Confucianism. The Meiji *genro* drew on a new enthusiasm for this in Japan in the late nineteenth century. The government of Singapore sought guidance from expatriate scholars of the tradition in the

3

United States in the 1970s. If those who lead the People's Republic of China into the next century are not content simply to think of themselves as Chinese, they may call on scholars of their own. Korea has been said to be the most Confucian society of all; even the Chinese used to call it 'the land of the superior man'. Those who see the Chinese societies in this way choose to ignore Confucius' own celebration of a golden age and his distaste for entrepreneurship, invert the long-standing inclination of Europeans to use his precepts to explain why nothing in Asia would change, and point to the energy that has come from the emphasis on self-cultivation, the common good and constructive rule. Outside the Chinese societies, the claims are different. In Thailand's political deference, some see the injunction in the country's Theravada Buddhism to accept one's subordination in order to give rulers the strength and spirit to rule. In Suharto's authority in Indonesia, some detect the long-standing reverence in Java for the leader who can ride the cycle of misfortune, reconcile opposites and contain his antagonists. The starting points vary, but the conclusions can be made to converge. East Asians, it is said, are disposed to favour harmony and order, and expect their rulers to secure it.

Not all observers accept a difference. A vice-minister at the Ministry of International Trade and Industry (MITI) in Tokyo once irritably remarked that east Asia is merely a place. Its societies, he said, have nothing in common. Some who do see difference refuse in a fashionably post-foundationalist manner to accept that it is grounded in anything other than talk about it. (In debate with Derrida, one intellectual in Japan went so far as to say that the long-standing capacity to combine old tropes with the new show Japan to have been post-modern before modernity.) Others have observed, like Clifford Geertz of Islam, that the beliefs which indicate the difference are relatively recent formulations of once unspoken cosmologies. This perhaps is closest to the truth. The reconstructions of 'Asian-ness' in the 1980s and 1990s, like those in the 1920s and 1930s, are the creations of self-serving politicians and their publicists. They are deployed in dislike of domestic dissent against the insistence of a divided and decadent West on the importance of liberalism and 'human rights'. As a history of textual precept and everyday practice, 'Asian-ness' is an undeniable, if elusive, fact; as a statement of principles, it is a modern artefact. The real difference between the West and east Asia is less a difference of principled beliefs than a difference between a world in which people have principled beliefs and a world in which they do not.

There is a new confidence in east Asia. But there is also unease. The pace of change in the region has been extra-ordinary. In few places in the twentieth century and nowhere in the past fifty years has the experience of successive generations been so different and often so painful. Because of this, because of the politics that in large part explains it and because of the ways in which the politics and their economic consequences have brought people in the region into contact with the West, the unease has extended to doubts about what 'east Asia' is and means. In Europe and north America, many still take it to be a single culture in a certain place. Even east Asians them-selves can do so. The more reflective sense that the issue is more complicated. They variously think of east Asia as a

5

bounded space, connected cultures, a single economy, a shared politics and a field of mutual security. To some, it is all of these. To others, it is none exactly. What is not in doubt is that it has been in constant flux and is changing now as quickly as it has ever done. It has for this reason first to be understood from its past.

III

The period in this past that connects to the present had existed for thousands rather than hundreds of years. It was the time in which 'east Asia' was the West's Orient, and the Orient China. China's was the largest economy in the world, the 'Middle Kingdom' of what the emperor's court in Peking regarded as a unified world of unilateral relations of tribute, 'gift' and private trade with the unenlightened in adjacent territories and islands to the east and south. The facts, of course, were always more complicated. China directly ruled the barbarians who were closest to it, indirectly ruled through appointing their local powers as its own officials, accepted more or less equal relations of trade with those at the periphery, and was indifferent to those beyond, for whom it cared little and had no hope. There were also lesser 'Middle Kingdoms'. Vietnam demanded tribute from Laos, Japan from Korea and Okinawa. Korea, which in the seventeenth century thought the new regime in China barbaric, for a while sought tribute from the Middle Kingdom itself. Even those from the West who wished to profit from east Asia had at first to adapt to the prevailing relations with a still suzerain China.

TRANSACTION RECORD

AT: CHAPTERS #772
    9631 MACLEOD TRAIL S
    CALGARY   AB
TERMINAL: 00247465   OPERATOR: 00000010
VISA: 4500 6078 1332 1   EXP 99/10
PURCHASE:

$ 14.41

AUTH. #:   005068   SWIPED
REFERENCE #:   2628   DATE: 99/09/02
BATCH #:   0641   TIME: 15:58:09
CARDHOLDER WILL PAY CARD ISSUER ABOVE
AMOUNT PURSUANT TO CARDHOLDER AGREEMENT

SIGNATURE:

        ROBERT S   JOHNSON
  HAVE A NICE DAY! BONNE JOURNEE!

(They often found these a puzzle. The United States consul in Seoul, who also advised the Korean king, was unable as late as the 1880s to tell Washington whether and in what sense one could speak of Korea as a sovereign state.)

But China was weakening. To sustain its advantage, it had started to fix prices in the Peking market below those prevailing in trade outside the country. It had also begun to pay in a paper currency, which inflated, rather than silver. Its reserves of silver were declining in value against the Europeans' gold. It was having to pay 'reparations' to foreign powers which reached crippling levels after its forced treaty with Japan in 1895. And although it was able to maintain monopolies outside China itself, imports were starting seriously to derange its economy. (It was in the middle of the century that it realized that it could no longer maintain its prohibition on migration and created what came to be an important diaspora.) The Meiji reformers decided that Japan should take the Middle Kingdom's place.

At the end of its war with China in 1894–5, Japan took Korea, Formosa (now Taiwan) and some smaller islands into a more formal and directive empire of its own. After the First World War, some in the Japanese army saw that the United States was assuming the power that Britain had once exercised against Asia, and came to believe that the next great conflict would be between Japan and the 'Anglo-Saxons'. They wished also to contain the new nationalism in China. (This was actually strongest, as the socialist Sun Yat-sen saw, in the diaspora.) They concluded that Japan must advance beyond trying to be the new China to become 'Asia's America', and fashioned a new and overtly

'Asian' aggressiveness to convince themselves. In 1931, the high command engineered the occupation of Manchukuo (Manchuria) in north-east China. That, however, drew Japan into a war with nationalists to the south. It was also costly. In 1939, desperate to recover what it could of its East Asia Co-Prosperity Sphere in the north-east, knowing that there were oil and other raw materials in the south-east, and taking courage from the fall of France, the military-directed government in Tokyo decided to extend the co-prosperity sphere and call it 'Great'. But Japan's shipping was quickly lost in the subsequent war and, by 1944, the United States' forces were closing on its home islands. Its attempt to become a world power had failed. Having made it, however, it was prepared to recover.

The European powers were eager after Japan's defeat to reclaim their colonies in the south-east. The British had soon to concede power in Burma. In Malaya, which politically and materially mattered to them more, they were able to re-establish their authority. So also, more precariously, were the Dutch in the East Indies and the French in Indochina. In the East Indies, nationalists had declared an Indonesian republic in the months between the Japanese surrender and the return of Dutch forces. The Dutch exploited the divisions between the nationalist factions and tried to restore their authority. But they had few funds, the United States had decided that Indonesia was less important than Indochina in the new Cold War, and it had been impressed by Sukarno's hostility at that time to the Indonesian Communist Party. In 1949, America persuaded them to withdraw and turned to support the French in Indochina against Ho Chi Minh's Viet Minh. It meanwhile saw no reason in 1945 not to keep the promise it had made ten years before to transfer power to the landed class in the Philippines, continued, with misgivings, to back the Kuomintang (KMT) against the Chinese communists, agreed, it said temporarily, to divide Korea with the Soviet Union and could not at first decide what to allow Japan to do. By 1948, it had accepted the fact of division on the Korean peninsula and the creation of two separate states. In 1949, the KMT was defeated on the mainland of China and its commanders had fled to Taiwan. In 1950, North Korea invaded the South. By 1952, China's retreat from the region (apart from North Korea) was complete.

Anticipating a state of affairs that it was itself doing much to create, the United States had already defined a 'great crescent' of defence around east Asia. In 1951, it sealed Japan's subordinate independence in a treaty of mutual security. Notwithstanding the prohibition on rearmament that the Americans had put into the country's new constitution in 1946–7, a clause which they (and only they) came later to regret, the United States had also persuaded the Japanese government to form a force for self-defence, accept its bases and turn a blind eye to the transit of nuclear weapons. It supported the revival of the country's industry to provide what one of its economic advisers described as a 'springboard and supply' for the war in Korea, which Prime Minister Shigeru Yoshida regarded as 'a gift from the gods'. Having revised its early enthusiasm for the radical 'democratization' of the country, it also endorsed Yoshida's construction of a conservative coalition in reaction to a newly unified left. America's new

Asia was centred in the north-east, and Japan was at its core.

The new east Asia soon extended. As early as 1947, at the very start of the Cold War, Dean Acheson had suggested that Japan should support the United States in Asia by providing capital and intermediate goods to the more fragile countries in the region; others in Washington added that this might also provide dollars for Europe. (The Ministry of Foreign Affairs in Tokyo had made a similar suggestion in 1946, although not for strategic reasons, and with no concern for Europe.) Yoshida disliked the idea. He returned from a journey to south-east Asia in 1954 to say that Japan should trade with rich men, not beggars. It was Nobusuke Kishi, Prime Minister in the Liberal Democratic Party's (LDP) coalition at the end of the 1950s, who made the move. Kishi had been a reforming civil servant in the Ministry of Commerce and Industry in the 1930s (the forerunner of the post-war Ministry of International Trade and Industry), had directed the industrialization of Manchukuo, and ran Commerce and Industry during the war. He saw that in gaining economic access to the south, Japan could meet America's wish and compensate for the break with China. Left-wing Asianists, hostile to the power of the United States, sympathetic to the new regime in China and indifferent to the south-east, were left to fret.

The anti-communist alliance lasted until the early 1970s, when, against everything it had been led to expect, Japan was caused to reconnect with China. The United States had come to see that it could not prevail in the war in Indochina, announced a policy of détente with the Soviet Union, decided to reduce its forces in east Asia, took the dollar off gold, which let the rest of the world's convertible currencies float and the yen rise, and imposed tariffs. It approached China to detach it further from the Soviet Union. Shocked by this rapprochement, and not a little humiliated by the way in which it was made (Washington had given what Henry Kissinger referred to as the 'small and petty book-keepers' in Tokyo just one hour's notice of the change), Prime Minister Kakuei Tanaka nevertheless overrode the opposition of the conservatives, including Kishi, who favoured Taiwan, and at once normalized Tokyo's relations with Beijing. He was sensitive to the fact that Japan's trade was already important to China and could again be important to Japan itself. He also hoped that those in the Chinese ruling group who had failed in their arguments for access to the West in order to offset the country's dependence on the Soviet Union might be strengthened by closer ties.

Following Kishi's move in the late 1950s, Tanaka's successors had already asked an eager MITI to extend aid to Indonesia, Thailand, Laos, Cambodia and South Vietnam and, with the United States, funded an Asian Development Bank. As Minister of Finance in the late 1960s, Tanaka used his powers against the conservatives to make arrangements for a guaranteed supply of oil and natural gas from Indonesia. These did not materialize, and the first oil-price rise in 1973 impelled Japan (notwithstanding its hasty diplomatic support of the Arab states) to take a wider view of its energy needs and accept the power of the American oil companies. But Indonesian oil continued to be important, and Indonesia and Thailand were beginning themselves to produce simple manufactures. The Ministry of Finance acknowledged the prospective benefit to Japanese firms and lifted its ban on overseas investment. The members of a new non-communist Association of South-east Asian Nations, many of whose leaders remembered the Japanese occupation little more than twenty years before, disliked what they saw as renewed interference in their economies and Japan's even-handed relations with China and the communist parties in Indochina. This resistance and the north's subsequent victory in Vietnam led Japan to see that it had to work for more co-operative relations between Japanese enterprises and those in the south-eastern economies, give more aid to the members of ASEAN than it was giving to China, acknowledge the association's importance for the security of the region (the purpose for which the association had been formed) and try to mediate with the communist powers.

The United States had nevertheless persuaded Japan to redefine the east Asia that it saw the two countries to be sharing as a wider 'Asia-Pacific'. America could thereby retain its influence, the south-east Asian states and China would be included, and Japan could continue to profit and assume more of the 'burden of leadership'. There was a corresponding proliferation of formal associations. The outcomes of their meetings, at least as these are reported, are famously empty; some regard them as little more than arenas of acquaintance. Their intention, however, shows what 'Asia–Pacific' is now thought by the Americans to be, and their extension shows how far they and the more powerful Asian states would now like it to extend. The first members of ASEAN had come together in 1967 in a shared experience of (in Thailand's case *de facto*) colonialism, a wish, as the war in Indochina escalated, to distance themselves from the United States, and a commitment to capitalism. By the mid-1990s, however, they had accepted Vietnam, Cambodia, Laos and Burma (whose military leaders had renamed it Myanmar). In 1989, Australia, acting on an idea it had been nurturing since the 1960s, initiated a forum for Asia–Pacific Economic Co-operation. APEC, including Canada and the United States as well as Brunei, Indonesia, Malaysia, Singapore, the Philippines, Thailand, South Korea, Japan, New Zealand and Australia itself, and extending later to Mexico, China, Taiwan, and Papua New Guinea, signalled an appreciation by most of the Asian countries (more acceptable in coming from Australia than from Japan or the United States) that their connections across the Pacific were as important as those with each other. From Malaysia, Mahatir retaliated by proposing a pointedly 'East Asian' Economic Grouping to balance the weight of the United States and China. But Washington, opposed to any association in Asia that excluded it, was hostile, Tokyo was embarrassed, the group became a mere 'caucus' ('without Caucasians', a wag observed) and soon died. In APEC's slipstream, the members of ASEAN turned their informal post-ministerial conference in 1993 into a Regional Forum on security whose 'dialogue partners' also include the United States and Canada as well as Japan, China, Russia, Australia, New Zealand, Papua New Guinea and even the European Union.

China's inclusion in this dialogue was more than a formal acknowledgement of Deng's succession to Mao. Political frontiers obscure the fact that in the matter of financial connections 'China' has been both of the republics that carry the name (when they meet in public, Taiwan is politely called China–Taipei) and Hong Kong as well. By the early 1990s, the combined value of exports and imports in the three Chinas exceeded that in Japan. They had between them accumulated foreign reserves that approached those of Japan, the United States and Germany combined. Enterprises in the People's Republic were receiving large amounts of foreign investment, and the government was receiving more than twice as much in foreign credits. Even though the subsequent economic expansion has hitherto been concentrated along the southern coast, the fact that this is the most naturally outward-looking region and the one that has the closest relations with emigrants beyond, together with the fact that China has been testing its new strength in contests over oil-bearing waters of interest to several south-east Asian states, makes it impossible now to ignore.

This is not to say that China has now displaced Japan at the centre of an expanding 'Asia–Pacific'. The value of its national product is still only about a tenth of Japan's, which is still about twice as large as those of China, South Korea, Taiwan and the ASEAN economies combined. Its average income per head (even when revised from the official figure, which was until recently depressed by unreal exchange rates) is less than an eighteenth of Japan's. And the new wealth along its southern coast has to be seen against increasing disparities with the interior. Japan's overseas holdings, which are now greater than those of any other country, have grown more quickly since the mid-1980s in Europe and the Americas (the United States has about half of the total) than in China. But China has been attracting prodigious amounts of money. In the first half of the 1990s there was a fivefold increase in inward investment in the country, 40 per cent of all the investment going to all the world's 'developing' countries, more than was going into any other country except the United States. China is also the largest recipient of loans from the multilateral banks, and still receives more aid than any other state. Its potential market gives it the power to secure proprietary technology from the West and its manufactures are becoming steadily more sophisticated. Its exports will probably continue to grow more quickly than its imports, and it may be able to turn its eventual membership of the World Trade Organization to its advantage. Some have accordingly been tempted to extrapolate its strength to a point at which, in a very different way, by a very different route and with entirely different relations to the rest of the world, it once again commands east Asia. Most, however, while acknowledging China's rise, accept that, in economic matters at least, Japan will dominate the region into the first quarter of the next century.

It is clear why even those who direct 'Asia–Pacific' and think in public about it disagree about its shape and what its distinctiveness consists in and practically implies. Like Europe, it contains divided histories and divided communities. Its present core has also been defined by economic ambition before the Second World War and the policy of the United States since. Unlike Europe, however, it has never had a dominant faith, and none to die for. Its political divisions have continued beyond the end of the Cold War, which was fought there, and there has been no comprehensive structure of mutual security. The region's economic transformation has been spectacular, but is not everywhere secure, and many of its corollaries in public and in private life have not so far been what liberals in the West might expect.

IV

In the 1980s and the first half of the 1990s, rates of economic growth in Japan settled to a modest average of around 3.5 per cent a year. In China, Hong Kong, Singapore, South Korea, Taiwan, Indonesia, Malaysia and Thailand (but not in the Philippines, Burma or the socialist states in the south-east) they were averaging between 5.5 and 10 per cent. By the early 1990s even the World Bank was prepared to talk of an 'east Asian miracle'. The miracle, however, had been rehearsed. In the late 1930s, a Japanese economist had plotted the progression over time of the substitution of domestic production for imports in a connected set of economies, and seen the shape of a skein of flying geese. The image took hold. In the 1970s, when Japan was taking seriously the United States' encouragement in the 1950s to think seriously about becoming the 'workshop of Asia', the flying geese were revived and redescribed in the language of the time as the 'catching-up product cycle'. The more recently industrializing economies, the Japanese politely implied, would eventually come abreast of the one in front. It was meanwhile 'necessary', a committee at the Ministry of Finance was still insisting in 1990, 'that what Japan used to do should be done by the Asian newly industrialising economies' (NIEs), Hong Kong,

South Korea, Taiwan and Singapore, and that 'what the Asian NIEs used to do should be done by the ASEAN countries': necessary, that is to say, to Japan itself.

In the early 1970s, Japanese direct investment in the NIEs was in low-technology, labour-intensive manufacturing, textiles and electrical machinery. In what have conventionally been referred to as the ASEAN-4, Indonesia, Malaysia, Thailand and the Philippines, this investment was in the primary sector (especially mining) and resource-intensive manufacturing. By the early 1980s, except in Indonesia, it was going into more sophisticated industries. After the steep rise in the yen in 1986, which reduced profits on exports and lowered interest rates, Japanese firms concentrated their investment into more sophisticated production still. Their investment in the NIEs, however, fell, in part because of rising wages in these countries, in part because their currencies were also appreciating, in part because they were graduating from the United States' Generalized System of Preferences and thereby ceasing to be attractive as platforms for re-export. Since 1992, Japanese firms have been investing more heavily in China. By the mid-1990s, foreign direct investment by the NIEs themselves in the ASEAN-4 and China had exceeded that from Japan, and investment from Thailand, Malaysia and the Philippines was starting to go into China, Laos and Vietnam. Japan's own cumulative direct investment in Asia in the mid-1990s was about one-third of its cumulative investment in the United States, a little more than three-quarters of that in Europe.

Japan's strategy for expansion has been simple. Sophisticated products do not have to be made in one place, and products are becoming more sophisticated all the time. Different constituents require different technologies and different kinds and degrees of expertise and skill. In the Japanese firms, the most complicated and demanding processes are completed in Japan itself, the less demanding in Korea, Taiwan, or Singapore and now also in Thailand or Malaysia, the least demanding in the Philippines or China. This is not, as some have said, a strategy to create a second Great East Asia Co-Prosperity Sphere. The intention is to increase Japan's exports to the United States and Europe. Inter-Asian exports, which include a great deal of capital and intermediate goods, many of them moving within firms, comprise about a third of all trade in the region; most of the remaining two-thirds is with economies beyond. (Of the larger Asian economies, only China and Indonesia were by the mid-1990s still selling more to Japan than to anywhere else.) Japan's trade surplus with the rest of Asia, therefore, is now larger than that with the United States; only China, Thailand and Malaysia do not presently run a deficit with it. The other Asian economies make up for theirs by exporting in their own name to north America and Europe. It is not surprising that for all these countries (China and Indonesia have their ambitions too) the one meeting in 1996 that matched the importance of APEC, with its connection to the United States, was the first of what was hoped to be a series of 'summits' with Europe.

On the face of it, the explanation for the strategy's success is as simple as the strategy itself. There are complementary 'comparative advantages' in the region. Propinquity reduces 'transaction costs' between the various parties, which fall even more as the economies grow in size. Above all, firms constantly respond to the most promising markets. One has to add a few more details, of course, about the sources of capital and its price, and the causes, always less easy to determine, of technical advance. But this still leaves one asking why this has been the strategy it has, and why it has succeeded so. The answer is more complex than an orthodox economics might allow. It lies in the economic history of Japan itself. There, as an official in the Ministry of Foreign Affairs once politely explained, the view has been that 'laissez-faire can't be recommended'. It is the 'careful utilization of market forces', he explained, that 'is always ideal'.

Once the Occupation authorities had allowed several of the pre-war family-owned holding companies in Japan, the *zaibatsu*, to reform, once the United States had generously (or perhaps fortuitously) set a favourable exchange rate with the dollar, once it had been agreed that economic growth had in good part to depend upon exports, and once the politically conservative coalition was secure, Yoshida's government decided on the direction of its economic policy. It would offer cheap and extended credit, derived in part from what remains an extraordinarily high rate of domestic savings, to encourage adequate investment. It would balance modest competition in the domestic market with protection for sales abroad, the first for efficiency, the second for economies of scale. And it would offer 'administrative guidance' on initial and continuing investment. There were exceptions, of course, and some mistakes and failures. (When MITI decided to expand the manufacture of motor vehicles, it supported Mazda but not the motorcycle manufacturer Honda. Mazda had to be rescued from near-collapse after the oil-price rise in 1973; Honda flourished without guidance or support. One of the most dramatic failures was the concerted attempt, costing some $100 million, to develop a 'fifth generation' of intelligent computers.) There were also prices to pay, for private consumers in Japan who paid dearly for both imports and home-produced goods, for the myriad small suppliers who received neither credit nor guidance and were at the mercy of their powerful customers, and in what economists call unproductive 'rents' in business and in government that arguably benefited few beyond those who extracted them. Nonetheless, the results in the twenty years of high growth in Japan to 1973 were spectacular.

This was not simply because of the government support for business. External conditions were also propitious. The demand for Japan's exports proved greater than anyone had expected. And there were other conditions within Japan itself, not least the distinctive relations within business itself and between business and labour. Big business consisted of extended networks of firms, *keiretsu*, in which the connections were much more than contingently contractual. Four of the six *keiretsu*, Fuji (formerly Fuyo), Mitsubishi, Sakura (formerly Mitsui) and Sumitomo, were pre-war *zaibatsu*. In the reconstruction, each was encouraged to regroup around a bank that would provide it with credit and other services. They held each other's shares, did not have to pay regular dividends to shareholders, and could take a long view. The two new networks, Daiichi Kangyo and Sanwa, were started from such banks. The firms in each network covered production and distribution, and their executives regularly met. In the late 1980s, when credit expanded, the relations loosened. But the *keiretsu* continue, and have since tightened their links with their once separate suppliers. Their relations with labour, predicated on an exchange of secure employment for loyalty and modest pay, are slowly changing, and the promised financial deregulation and a rapidly ageing population will quicken the change. The ties nevertheless continue, and are peculiar to Japan.

In the 1970s, at the end of the period of fastest growth, the *keiretsu* were generating surpluses that were more than sufficient for their existing needs. They began to cease to need credit and to consider where next to move. They could repay their debts to the banks, diversify at home, speculate in securities and land, increase their spending on research and development or invest abroad. To repay made little sense; it was not clear to whom their banks would relend if they did. To diversify would be disruptive and in a changing market risky too, as those who attempted it were to see. To speculate would be idle, and could, as it did, rebound; there was a huge bubble at the end of the 1980s, the bursting of which has had lasting effects in bad debts on land and construction. (The Nippon Telegraph and Telephone Corporation was at one point in the madness nominally valued at more than the whole of West Germany, the 300 acres of the imperial palace in central Tokyo at more than the state of California. The nominal debt of Japanese National Railways alone was greater than those of the states of Brazil and Mexico combined.) To increase spending on research and development, by contrast, made excellent sense. Given the appreciation of the yen, rising wages at home, the pressures on the trade surplus with the United States and the need to exploit the results of new research and development, together with increasing opportunities in the increasing number of potential recipients, firms saw that they also had to produce more abroad.

In making their overseas investments, Japanese firms have extended their connections with each other. They remain multi- rather than trans-national corporations; strategic decisions are taken at the headquarters in Japan, not devolved. In their operations in other countries, Japanese managers work alongside those they recruit locally, and in their dealings with locals and their suppliers extend the same embrace, and the same disciplines, as they have at home. (Toyota was loyal to its suppliers, but became famous for fining them $1,500 for every minute they were late with a shipment.) The government in Tokyo supports the move by extending low-interest loans to smaller suppliers that are willing to make it. It covers at least 90 per cent of the losses incurred by any firm abroad through unforeseen circumstances of a commercial or political kind. It offers guidance both in Tokyo and through its attachés to the other Asian capitals. This is sometimes technical, on the practicalities, for instance, of buying into telecommunications in the region, sometimes tactical, on how, for example, to pay the correct amount of 'tea-money' to foreign governments. (Japanese firms are not in this respect bound by restrictive legislation, and have in some cases made considerable outlays. They are thought to have given about $50 million in the 1980s to the venal Marcos regime in the Philippines.) The government also supports a programme to train foreign workers in Tokyo.

The connections between Japanese firms and the Japanese government and between both of these and firms and governments in the countries in which Japan invests are not unnaturally seen in different ways. 'We have a very strong rapport with the government,' the Japanese manager of Matsushita's air conditioner plant in Malaysia once remarked. 'Whenever we have a problem, we contact them and work it out. We feel as though we have married Malaysia. We love the government, we love the people.' The government in Kuala Lumpur is less fulsome, but in spite of the financial concessions it has had to make, takes the same view. Malaysian businessmen, by contrast, frequently resent the control that Japanese firms are careful to maintain. There are similar differences of opinion in other countries. But the recipients of private investment from Japan (and of the Overseas Development Assistance that is offered from Tokyo in the hope that it will increase connections) know that they need the Japanese. Weak civil law, high levels of economic and political risk and the sheer opacity of their societies often make it difficult for them to attract sufficient investment from elsewhere; and when the money does come, it is often difficult to make it work so well.

Japan's own economy, however, has suffered a recurring cycle in the past twenty years, and in the late 1990s it has been finding it difficult to escape from near recession. The yen tends to fall against the dollar, making exports cheaper and prompting the trade surplus with the United States to rise. The United States reacts, which causes the yen to rise. In the second half of 1995, the yen began to fall again. For reasons of its own, the American economy was stronger than it had been on previous occasions, and the Americans were less irritated than before by Japan's surplus. For reasons also of its own, Japan had less room than previously in which to manoeuvre. In the past, it has bought more United States Treasury bonds to finance that country and increased its domestic spending. In 1997, faced with a large budget deficit, it reduced its domestic expenditure and raised a sales tax that it had introduced to alleviate fiscal difficulty in 1989. Interest rates are low, but so is new investment. In 1997, two large securities firms and a bank, the tenth largest, were allowed to fail; the Fuji bank, breaking with precedent, refused to support the securities firm in its group. After some hesitation, the government provided considerable surplus liquidity and even itself offered loans to prevent further collapses. In the longer run, everything will turn on the government's success in deregulating Japan's expensive distribution and energy industries, further reducing the financial support to what (before Prime Minister Morihiro Hosokawa's reform of the electoral system in 1994) had been the Liberal Democrats' invaluable supporters in agriculture, and open- ing its financial markets. The far-sighted in Japan itself, as well as commentators from the West, are convinced that the costs of the protection it has provided to its firms and farmers are not sustainable. Nor, if the economy is to move again, is the machinery of regulation itself. Not for nothing, perhaps, is Prime Minister Ryutaro Hashimoto so keen of a morning to practise his swordplay on the roof of the MITI building. He is committed to the reform of embedded defences, and he knows that this will not be easy.

Japan's recurring difficulty is a function of the success and subsequent strength of the structure that served it so well into the 1980s. It has net credits of $350 billion. Its foreign reserves, of about $200 billion, are more than twice those of Germany and three times those of the United States. Its business corporations remain among the most secure and sophisticated in the world, and the most powerful. In the mid-1990s, only eight or nine of South Korea's large firms and two or three of Taiwan's were included in *Fortune* magazine's top 500. There were none from the rest of Asia. In Japan, by contrast, there are nearly as many, about 150, as in the United states. Japan also has the largest banks. Although it has important economic interests outside Asia, and although its government may, as an official from MITI has put it, have no 'policy on regionalism', the regional policy that it does admit to, a policy of investment, aid and trade to sustain its rate of accumulation, has been designed to maintain its dominance in what is still the fastest growing part of the world. And this, some in Japan itself are pleased to note, will have been strengthened by the downturn in 1997 in the economies in the south-east. Few doubt that, whatever Japan's more immediate difficulties, its success in east Asia is assured into at least the first quarter of the next century.

The growth in the wider region, striking though it is, has not matched that of Japan itself in the 1960s or of South Korea in the 1970s. But with the exceptions of Botswana and Mauritius, both small economies, none anywhere in the world grew as quickly in the years between 1980 and the mid-1990s as did those of China, Hong Kong, Indonesia, South Korea, Malaysia, Singapore, Taiwan and Thailand. (In the 1980s, Burma, Cambodia, Laos and Vietnam were recovering, where they were not still suffering, from internal wars, and even in the late 1990s each has yet to commit itself to a wholly open economic strategy. It is only the Philippines which suffered a negative rate of growth – of just over half of 1 per cent – over these fifteen years, and which still has a per-capita income lower than any of the more successful economies except Indonesia, that cannot thus be explained away.) In the light of the fast growth, it did not seem unreasonable in the mid-1990s for an informed observer in the United States to suggest that, with surpluses on their current accounts, 'low labour costs, adequate technology, improving infrastructure, and a pool of increasingly affluent consumers', their future was assured.

Such are the hazards of economic prediction. By the second half of 1997, only Singapore, of the seven more successful economies, was not facing a rising deficit on its current account, an unstable currency, falling imports and reduced investment. In 1995, all seven had been enjoying their highest rates of growth in exports for a decade. The yen was exceptionally strong, and exporters could profitably sell (or sell back) to Japan itself. But then the yen began to fall. This left the six with rising stocks and falling incomes. At the same time, a drop in the demand for electronic goods caused the price of semiconductors from China, Malaysia, Singapore, South Korea and Taiwan to collapse. (In 1995, South Korea was selling DRAM semiconductors at $13.50; by late 1996, the price was $5.00.) Two events, a downturn in Japan's cycle and a fall in demand for an important part of the other economies' production, had coincided. Meanwhile, private money had been pouring into poorly-regulated banks, which in turn lent foolishly, often, in Thailand and Indonesia, to finance politicians, in Malaysia, to finance more public extravagance. Traders who had hitherto assumed that real growth was assured in the region suddenly decided that the Thai baht, the Malaysian ringgit and the Indonesian rupiah were overvalued, receiving too much support from short-term loans, too little from the real economy, and sold.

The cyclical coincidence and the traders' reaction exposed some deeper difficulties. The first was in the relations between Japan's currency and those of the other Asian economies. Much of the direct investment in these economies has come from Japan; their sales are increasingly to the United States and Europe. Their currencies have accordingly tended to shadow the dollar, with the result that when the yen falls their cost advantages are reduced and their exports start to compete with those from Japan and China. Some in Japan have wanted them to shadow the yen. This would stabilize Japan's own trade with the rest of Asia, denominate less of it in dollars, and perhaps increase the yen's presently faint attractions as a reserve currency. 'We need a regional group,' Eisuke Sakakibara, the vice-minister for international finance in the Ministry of Finance, has said. 'The European single currency is coming, and the North Atlantic Free Trade Area [NAFTA] is growing, so we need co-operation in Asia.' But this is delicate. It could threaten the United States. After

1997, however, commentators wonder whether in the event of another economic crisis in the region the drain on the funds of a regional group might be too much to bear; economies there are now too vulnerably synchronized. Hashimoto, talking now of cranes, not flying geese, remarked that for the moment, Japan does not presently have the strength to lead, and looks to the IMF and the United States.

A second difficulty exposed by the downturn in 1997, a difficulty that has affected Thailand, Indonesia and some production in China (and will affect Vietnam and Cambodia in the future), is that the advantages these economies have had in the production of labour-intensive goods, of textiles, garments, plastic goods and easily assembled electrical products, are diminishing. In many cases, the raw materials have to be imported, and the prices of many, like the prices of intermediate and foreign consumer goods, have been rising. At the same time, competition from other economies in which wages are low, in central and eastern Europe, central Asia and Latin America, is becoming more intense.

The prospect would not be so severe if the poorer economies in east Asia were securely placed in the 'catching-up product cycle'. But they are not. The technologically most advanced production in both the NIEs and the ASEAN countries is largely in firms using technology from Japan. One might suppose, from the conventional wisdom, that this would in time transfer to firms in the less advanced economies. Japanese firms certainly transport their high technology to the sites of production. But they do not transfer it. The technology gap between Japan and the other economies has been increasing, and Japanese corporations admit that this is what they intend. Only China, with the economic power to extract proprietary technology from the West, is in a different position.

This might not be so serious if the smaller economies were investing adequately in the infrastructure that is necessary to grow and in the research and development to make it possible to do so by increasing the productivity of their own firms. But again, and unlike China, they are not. The supply of energy and the ease of transport and communication in these countries has not been keeping up with the pace of growth; indeed, investment in these was already falling slightly in the early 1990s and was brought to a virtual standstill in the devaluations of 1997. In South Korea and Taiwan as well as the ASEAN countries, levels of spending on research and development have been at about 1 per cent of the value of sales from manufacturing, less than a half of the comparable proportion in Japan itself. Only in Taiwan and Singapore (which has recently announced that it also wants to attract qualified foreigners to settle) are there plans to raise it.

In many parts of the south-east and in China, levels of education too are poor. In Malaysia, slightly more than half the relevant age-group was receiving any secondary education at the beginning of the 1990s. In Indonesia and Thailand, the proportion was little more than one-third. Outside the NIEs, it is only in the Philippines that it was more than three-quarters. It was only in the Philippines and Malaysia that the proportion was greater than that which had been receiving any secondary education in South Korea in 1970. In Thailand, by contrast, where gross domestic product per head in 1992 was about the same as it had been in Taiwan in 1978 or in South Korea in 1984, only 37 per cent of the age-group were in secondary education, compared with 94 per cent in Taiwan and 91 per cent in Korea in the earlier years. The example of the Philippines (with Sri Lanka and most of Latin America) does, it is true, make it clear that widespread secondary education is not sufficient. The Philippines' GDP per capita in the early 1990s was only slightly more than a third of Thailand's, slightly more than a quarter of Malaysia's. But few doubt that it helps. Only in Singapore, where the government has consistently tried to improve levels of skill, does the proportion of growth attributable to increases in productivity, rather than to the application of additional capital and labour, reach more than half. It is for these reasons that what has been happening in the area has been described as 'ersatz capitalism', the economies there as 'paper tigers'.

Yet even if they are, and even if their growth is for a few years set to fall from the high levels of the later 1980s and early 1990s, their prospects may not be quite as bleak as some suggest. It is true that Japanese firms have recently been hesitating, but they will continue to need to export their production, and will continue to find it easier to export it to east Asia. Investments in Europe and north America may be necessary to circumvent the barriers that have been raised by the European Union and NAFTA. But these barriers may be lowered if the United States and Europe are able to hold each other to account under the extended rules of international trade that were agreed at the end of the final round of the General Agreement on

Tariffs and Trade in 1993 and are now enshrined in the World Trade Organization. It is only in east Asia that Japanese firms can have the kind of support they like to have from their government, and only there that they can operate through the *jinmyaku*, the 'veins of humanity', that suit them so well. Enterprises from outside Asia may also continue to be attracted to the lower-cost economies in the south-east, although investment in Vietnam, Cambodia, Laos and Burma/Myanmar has not so far been great; the governments (and, in the case of Burma/Myanmar, concerted international disapproval) do not yet make it easy. The biggest threat to the south-east Asian economies will come from 'Greater China'. Large foreign reserves have forestalled devaluations there. Investment from Japan has been increasing. Vice-premier Zhu Rongji's announcement to the fifteenth Party Congress in 1997 that the People's Republic itself would take steps to liberalize the loss-making state-owned heavy industries (and thereby free banks from much bad debt) will attract new ventures for capital and intermediate goods, and for export.

It is in Indonesia and the two Koreas that the structural problems are perhaps most immediately acute. Indonesia faces low prices for oil and declining reserves, has been losing capital-intensive investment to other countries in the south-east, has accumulated huge foreign debt in a recently expanded, poorly regulated and highly politicised private banking system, does not, unlike Thailand or Malaysia, have a competent and relatively uncorrupt civil service, and with the now ill and elderly Suharto's decision to run again for president in 1998 (with the economically nationalist Habibie as his vice-presidential running mate) faces political uncertainty. Its economy will take longer to recover than any other in east Asia. In Korea, the Democratic People's Republic in the north appears unable now even reliably to feed its own people. Commentators have long been saying that 'it is only a matter of time' before it will be forced towards a greater opening. In the late 1990s, they may at last be right, but the Republic to the south will want to take advantage of that. Profitability there has declined with rising wages and other costs since the 1980s, too little has been spent on research and development, and, unlike those in Taiwan, its firms are heavily financed by loans, which has increased the country's overall debt and weakened its financial institutions. An investment-led boom in 1995 produced over-capacity and fall in export prices. Firms responded by taking short-term loans from abroad, but as the downturn deepened, repayments became difficult, lenders refused to reschedule, the country's credit rating fell, and default threatened on what was now US$100 billion of short-term debt. Fearful of the likely impact on Japanese banks, which held US$25 billion of Korean debt, and of wider repercussions, the United States backed support from the IMF at the end of 1997 more extensive than any in the Fund's history. All of the east Asian economies will record lower rates of growth for 1997. South Korea's will be lower than that in any year since the disastrous 1980.

V

Japan and China are the only countries in east Asia to come into the region's new economy with an industry created under another. (The third and last to do so will be North Korea.) In South Korea, much of the industry and infrastructure that the Japanese had put in place during their occupation was destroyed in the war in 1950–3. (In North Korea, this industry was temporarily taken underground.) In Taiwan, the Philippines, Thailand and the European colonies in the south-east there were merely a few textile factories and food-processing plants. Where industry in most of east Asia did not have to start again, in these countries, it had to start from scratch. Agriculture of course did not. But either because the Japanese before the war (or various reformers after it, including the Chinese Communist Party, the Americans, the North Koreans and the KMT) forced a redistribution of land or because, as in Thailand, there had not been a landed class to displace, farming since the 1950s has everywhere except in the Philippines been largely in the hands of small farmers. Almost none of the new east Asian societies came into the 1960s with a politically entrenched business or landed class.

The political fortunes of these societies have also been affected by war and civil strife. In Korea, the conflict that began in 1950 with the North's invasion of the South ended three years later (more or less exactly on the line that had divided the two new states at the start) with no formal peace. The North Vietnamese won their thirty-year war in 1975 and unified the country, but China, angered

33

by Vietnam's attack on its Cambodian ally three years later, engaged it on its northern border. In Cambodia itself, a five-year civil war resulted in the victory in 1975 of the revolutionary Khmer Rouge. It was this that had prompted the invasion by a Vietnam that had been anxious, it claimed, to resist threats from 'the tiger in the woods' to the north. In Laos, conflict was sharpened by the United States' determination to defeat the former North Vietnam and was only ended (save for a brief and bloody border war with Thailand in 1987) by the establishment of a People's Democratic Republic in 1975. In Indonesia, Suharto's New Order was constructed on the breakdown in 1965 of Sukarno's precarious dependence on both the armed forces and the Communist Party and a subsequent massacre of many thousands of communist supporters. Conflict has subsided since the end of the Cold War in the West. But in Burma, civil war between the government and ostensible secessionists in the north, driven by anger against Rangoon and the profits to be made from drugs, persisted into the early 1990s. There is sporadic resistance in the 1990s in the Philippines and in northern Sumatra, the former Portuguese colony of East Timor and a scattering of Indonesia's other islands.

In the continuation of internal war and the absence of powerful interests in land and business, many of the formerly colonial countries of east Asia have resembled those in Africa more than most in the rest of Asia or in Latin America. The military have exercised power not because they favour one class or coalition of classes over another, but because, outside the Philippines, there have been no established classes to favour. They have also been strengthened by the support, political, financial, material and logistic, of one or other of the great powers. In the late 1990s, they still exercised absolute power in Burma/Myanmar and remained influential, perhaps decisive, in North Korea, Indonesia and Thailand. Only in Japan, Malaysia and Singapore have they remained altogether outside politics. What one cannot say of east Asia, however, which John Lonsdale has nicely said of Africa, is that its 'most distinctive contribution to the history of humanity has been the art of living in a reasonably peaceful way without the state'. The institutionalized practice of authoritative public power has existed for longer in China than anywhere else, and was established in the territories of what are now Laos, Cambodia, Vietnam, parts of Indonesia, Korea and Japan before Europeans and north Americans arrived. It is from this past that those aspiring to power in the post-war period have been able successfully to use 'national security' and the need for reconstruction and growth to claim an exclusive authority.

They have from time to time, it is true, appeared to put this authority to the test. There were formal contests for power at the ballot box as early as 1946 in the Philippines and Thailand, 1947 in Japan, 1948 in South Korea and 1951 in Burma. There were post-colonial elections in 1955 in Cambodia, Indonesia and Malaya, in 1958 in Laos, in 1959 in Singapore (then still part of Malaya), and from the 1970s in Taiwan. But with the exceptions of the election of weak coalitions in Thailand in 1973 and 1993 and the setback to the ruling LDP in Japan between 1993 and 1996, which in 1997 had still not recovered its overall majority, there have been no clear and unforced transfers of power anywhere in the region. The Socialist Cabinet that came to power in Japan in 1947 stood down under pressure from the American Occupation in 1948; the conservative coalition has governed, with interruption in the mid-1990s, ever since. The Philippines has been a quarrelsome oligarchy of landowners; this collapsed into martial law in 1972 (Marcos having rebelled at the refusal to allow him to run for a third term) and, after a moment's popular enthusiasm, re-emerged in much the same condition in 1986. The civilian government that was elected in Burma in 1960 (the elections there in 1951, 1956 and 1960 have been the only constitutionally ordained sequence in east Asia outside Japan) was overthrown by the military in 1962. The civilian governments that were elected in Laos in 1958 and Thailand in 1975 were thrown out within a few months. The government that was elected in Cambodia in 1955 was undermined by an American coup in 1968. The government that was elected in Indonesia in 1955 (the only free election that Indonesia has had and arguably the most open of any in south-east Asia since the Second World War) was subverted four years later, in the name of a new Guided Democracy, by the man who had led it. Most bizarrely perhaps, the military State Law and Order Restoration Council in Burma/Myanmar held what observers claimed were 'free and fair' elections in 1990 and then proceeded to prevent the National League for Democracy, which won them, from exercising its authority. Syngman Rhee did lose in elections to the South Korean National Assembly in 1958, which after his final humiliation in 1960 by the exposure of one last act of political violence endorsed a new government that lasted for just one hundred days. But not until 1997 was there a peaceful transfer of power to an opposing party in that country, and since 1965 there have not been any transfers of power at all in Indonesia, Malaysia, Singapore, Taiwan or Vietnam. The fact that some of these states have had formally liberal constitutions (and often several) is therefore meaningless. The only such constitution that has remained unchanged and been formally enforced is the one that was imposed on Japan by General MacArthur and his aides in 1946–7.

One cannot therefore read much into these elections. Like many of their counterparts elsewhere, those in power in east Asia stage such contests in order to ensure that their rule is acceptable to those who expect government to depend on the popular vote; to expose and hopefully to undermine those opponents who might consider opposing them in other ways; formally to accept that their power depends on the people and theatrically to show that it does not. Unlike some governments elsewhere, however, those in east Asia scarcely even pretend to govern on behalf of a sovereign people. They rule, and in ruling, presume that it is more important to be seen to be good men than to uphold the law. This is why they rarely offer principled justifications for what they do. They do exercise their rule through bureaucracies, and, because these perform much the same range of functions as state bureaucracies elsewhere, they might be thought to have been instituted in these countries for much the same reasons. Once again, however, a superficial similarity masks a subtle but decisive difference. In western Europe, state bureaucrats are civil servants, serving the state, as the term suggests, on behalf of the citizens. In the United States, they serve the state on behalf of the party in power. In east Asia, they serve a state that has seen itself as both principal and agent.

The origins of modern bureaucracy in Asia are in the politically disputatious first two decades of the Meiji. Factions there fought, and the authority of whoever happened to hold office was perpetually in question. One solution to the uncertainty was to submit to public opinion. The other was to confer absolute sovereignty on the emperor and declare that he, not the public, embodied the national interest. The first was pressed by those in a People's Rights Movement and the nascent political parties, who looked to Great Britain and the United States, the second by the *genro*, who sent one of their number, Ito Hirobumi, to Prussia, were cheered by his reports and won. They rejected the idea of state and society as separate spheres, excluded the parties, connected the emperor to the national interest and decided that he should be served by a bureaucracy whose quality would be determined in competitive examination (or by the mere fact of graduation, Ito decided, from the new Tokyo Imperial University) and so ensure that the national interest was met.

Ito had been clear. 'The state', he observed in 1888, the year before these measures were given constitutional effect, 'will eventually collapse if politics are entrusted to the reckless discussions of the people.' The architects of a modernizing Siam in the 1890s, the leaders of the new South Korea and Taiwan in the early 1950s and those who came to power later in the 1950s and in the 1960s in Malaysia, Singapore and Indonesia took the point. They followed the Japanese model. In the socialist states, the conception, and thus the practice, was different; it followed the Soviet elision of state and party. Only the oligarchy in the Philippines followed the Americans. The Japanese model has been an excellent instrument with which to contain dissent, please the military at home and powers abroad and reconstruct and direct the economy. It is true that in Japan in the Occupation after 1945, in Thailand, in the post-colonial states, even, by the mid-1980s, in the garrison states of Taiwan and South Korea, pressures from within and without made it necessary to adapt it to the form, if not the spirit, of the democracy that Ito had so disliked. But, since the disposition was to form an unassailable ruling party, since new constitutions were instituted in such a way as to minimize the possibility of power being transferred to another, and since those in politics, the law, business and usually the military as well were able to rely on the 'veins of humanity' that informally connected them, the bureaucracies and the political class were able together to retain their power.

Indonesia and Thailand reveal what is at stake in moving, as many outside the region and a handful of intellectuals within it have hoped, to democracy of a more Western, liberal kind. Except in its reduction of poverty, Indonesia is the least developed of the larger states in the region. Its civil service is over-manned, under-educated, politicized and corrupt, a poor instrument for the implementation of government policy. For the formulation of this policy, Suharto accordingly depended on his 'Berkeley mafia', a small group of American-trained economists who were responsible to him directly and to whom he gave a free hand. They were able to take drastic action to end high inflation and ensure that the objective of a balanced budget was put into the constitution in 1967, to manage the collapse of the national oil company, Pertamina, in 1975 (a collapse that affected 50,000 employees and left a debt of 40 per cent of the country's national income), to liberalize the economy after the fall in the price of oil in 1986, and to make sure that the conditions that have been set by the IMF and the World Bank, most recently in 1997, are met. At the same time, the President has had to rely on clients. Several of these, his children, to whom he has granted generous concessions, businessmen from the Chinese community, who have done extremely well through licences to market basic foodstuffs, and the adventurous Professor Habibie, whom Suharto tempted back from the aviation industry in Germany to develop high-technology industries in Indonesia, depend on his person. The military's power to extract favours may now be on the decline. Their involvement (in the name of their declared 'twin function' of protecting the revolution and the republic) in state enterprises and in putting down resistance is now seen to have been malign, and their presence suits Suharto's foreign supporters less than it did.

Institutional power in Indonesia lies in the government party, Golongan Karya, 'functional groups', known everywhere as Golkar. This controls the day-to-day administration of the larger part of the society through its incorporation of the only permissible associations of civil servants, businessmen, farmers, labour, the professions, women and youth, and its appointment of village headmen. It is also the only accepted channel of complaint.

Religious associations are independent, although it is Habibie, not noted for his faith, who directs the Indonesian Association of Muslim Intellectuals, the most influential patronage network of Islamic bureaucrats, professionals and businessmen. The two parties that are allowed legally to oppose Golkar are fiercely constrained. The only secular associations that escape its control are non-governmental, and these are either encouraged to become commercial or prevented from extending their reach. In these respects, Indonesia resembles the formerly communist party-states, and is similarly fragile. There is no obvious successor to the elderly Suharto, and it is not at all clear (especially if there is popular discontent at the material consequences of the devaluation in 1997 and the IMF succeeds in insisting that the foodstuffs and high-technology industries be deregulated) that his highly personal and politicized institutions can survive him. There may be a change in the rules of rule themselves, but, if this is to a more openly competitive democracy, no one can yet see how this might work. Without an established, competent and reasonably impersonal administration, it is not easy to see how it could.

The regime in Thailand, by contrast, even though the details of its constitutions are regularly rewritten, is secure. It is governments that are not. The Thai bureaucracy, unlike that in Indonesia, is professional and relatively efficient. It was not, however, constructed to protect a political class from internal feuds, popular will or the army. Civil governments in Thailand characteristically combine professional politicians, ex-army officers and a large number of local political bosses who get elected to the

Assembly by dispensing patronage to rural electors. The instability lies in the fact that these men form the majority and so choose the government and are opposed by the urban middle class and the army, who have repeatedly used coups to bring their administrations down. This circus, in which those who bring governments in in Thailand are not usually those who take them out, turns on the wide difference between the more developed cities and the countryside. It took a particularly violent turn in the 1970s. A strengthened military government (formed, like several others in the Third World at that time, by a coup within a coup) lost its credibility when the United States (again without warning) changed its policy toward China. Unprecedented demonstrations in the autumn of 1973, at one point bringing half a million people on to the streets of Bangkok, an interim regime, which allowed equally unprecedented liberties and constitutional revision, a new government dominated by politicians of the left, and an extra-parliamentary mobilization from the right three years later (frightened by what was happening in Thailand itself and by the victories of left-wing forces in Vietnam, Laos and Cambodia) eventually ended in another coup. Optimists now hope that the middle class and the military (whose power has in any event declined) might come to acknowledge the material grievances of those in the countryside. The strongest grounds for this may lie in the end of the Cold War and, more enduringly, in the fact that in Thailand, as in Japan, competitive electoral politics did not emerge until the bureaucracy had already established a monopoly on what the state could deliver. The price of the present competition and of the corruption on which it depends is all but irremediably weak financial control. India, one might say, is a picture of Thailand's hope, Pakistan of its fear.

Yet whatever the differences in their pasts, and whatever difficulties each may have experienced during the Cold War, one might expect the east Asian countries to become more 'democratic' as they become more prosperous. The moves to what appears to be a more open competition since the mid-1980s in the now 'developed' South Korea and Taiwan can suggest this. They have certainly been moves from a very different past. Kim Jong-pil had led a group of classmates from the military academy into a military coup in South Korea in 1961. Too young to take power publicly, these men accepted Park Chung-hee, an older relative of Kim's, as their leader. Park had risen in the Japanese Kwantung Army and come to admire what the colonial power had done. His junta set out to imitate it. By 1971, however, there were difficulties. The IMF had put a cap on loans to the large corporations, the United States had stopped paying for the use of Korea's men and *matériel* in Vietnam, and a civilian opponent, Kim Dae-jung, had nearly defeated Park in a presidential election. The President accordingly revised the constitution to constrain the opposition and allow his perpetual re-election by an electoral college. He was shot dead at dinner one evening eight years later by the chief of the Korean Central Intelligence Agency, who said that he thought Park had gone too far. A new coup brought Chun Doo-hwan, also from military intelligence, into the presidential Blue House. Chun set a limited term for the presidency and then suspended his new constitution to rule through a Legislative National

Security Council. (He even had Kim Dae-jung kidnapped and brought back to a sentence of death; the United States persuaded him to relent.) What undid Chun was his insistence at the end of his term in 1987 that his successor be chosen by the electoral college and his choice, as that successor, of Roh Tae-woo, the marine general who had secured Seoul for him in 1980. Demonstrations in the capital by students and a large number of white-collar workers, together with pressure once again from the United States, which was now embarrassed by being seen to support such a regime, forced Roh to abandon his friend and make another constitutional change. This inaugurated South Korea's Sixth Republic.

A divided opposition allowed Roh's popular election in 1987. The ruling party lost its majority in the National Assembly the following year, but by 1990 Roh had successfully extended this party by persuading two of the three which opposed it to join. One of the leaders of this erstwhile opposition was elected to the presidency in 1992; it had been a condition of his joining that he should stand. By 1997, the ruling group was divided by charges of corruption and other matters and the economy was in trouble. Its old adversary, Kim Dae-jung, accordingly decided to stand again in the presidential election at the end of the year and, against a discredited and divided right, won. In Taiwan, the ruling KMT lifted martial law in 1987 and opened itself to electoral competition. The opposition failed in the first open presidential contest in 1996, but it is thought that the popular mayor of Taipei, Chen Shui-ban, a man who served a spell in prison for his liberal views, could consolidate it for the next and win.

These histories can be told, and have been, as stories of inceasing liberalization under pressure from increasingly numerous, prosperous, well-educated and internationally more sensitive middle-classes. But the ruling parties in each country remain less parties in the Western sense than coalitions of factions fuelled by large amounts of cash and brought together by a desire for power and a distaste for popular dissent. In the presidential elections in Taiwan in 1996, the KMT wished to engineer a succession from the son of the KMT's first leader to a native Taiwanese. Widely agreed now to be the richest ruling party in the world, the party managed without difficulty to co-opt a number of factions from the opposition, which was as divided on the issues, including the question of the country's relations with China, as the KMT itself. In the run-up to the presidential election in South Korea in December 1997, Kim Dae-jung's party came to an arrangement with Kim Jong-pil. On his return from financial disgrace under Chun (the simplest way for a Korean to despatch an influential enemy), Kim Jong-pil prepared the ground for Roh's coalition in 1990; he offered the electorate an assurance of continuity and Kim Dae-jung votes from a region south of Seoul, in return for which he expected to hold Defence or Foreign Affairs. Park Tae-joon, the architect of Korea's successful steel industry whom Roh made chairman of the new coalition party in 1990, demanded a pardon for Roh and Chun, who were themselves financially disgraced; he brought votes from the east and expected to be rewarded with Economy. But in neither South Korea nor Taiwan, nor in Singapore, where the ruling party, although it holds regular elections and is not corrupt, consistently suppresses information and harasses the opposition, nor in Malaysia, where Malays, especially in the middle class, have benefited from discrimination in their favour since 1971, have electors shown any great inclination to move to what the Malaysian Prime Minister calls 'fanatical liberal democracy'. They value the order and stability which they believe guarantees their prosperity and pre-empts the civil strife that they, or their parents, have known.

'Call it the Sat-Cho government [the Satsuma-Choshu clique government],' one of those involved in the reforms in Japan remarked in 1881, 'or designate it by whatever name you wish; but who would deny its achievement in maintaining the security and well-being of 40 million souls.' This is a sentiment from which, a hundred years later, few in non-communist east Asia would demur. If they are changing their opinion, they are doing so slowly. It is conceivable that the change in Japanese politics since 1993, in which voters have been less inclined to support the LDP and in which factions within the party have been disposed to form others, indicates a greater responsiveness to urban consumers and to wider problems in the economy. It is even conceivable that Kim Dae-jung could be in a position to keep his promise to take South Korea from a presidential to a parliamentary regime by 2000. The hitherto complacent and corrupt political classes may be starting to accept that they have at least to appear to be more accountable.

VI

There is no doubt that, in consolidating the states that they rule, the political classes in non-communist east Asia have been greatly helped by the support in finance, trade, military preferment and intelligence that their predecessors received in the Cold War. Those in the communist states have been helped too, although several had to contend with the antagonism between the Soviet Union and China, and they all have now to rely on foreign capital and ASEAN. In both sets of countries, the end of the Cold War was less significant than in Europe. China's leaders had already drawn their conclusions from the fatal confusion of economic and political reform in the Soviet Union in the 1980s. Japan was preoccupied with the downturn in its economy in the later 1980s and by the political argument that had been started by American pressure to contribute to the defence of Kuwait in 1991. Taiwan, the south-east Asian nations and the United States were uneasy about China. Beijing had succeeded in diverting international recognition away from Taipei, but remained anxious about the moves that were being made there to declare a final and formal separation from the mainland and was insisting on *de facto* sovereignty over islands that are believed to be in oil-bearing waters. In 1989, it also did great damage to its international standing in overreacting to demonstrations in front of the Western press in Tiananmen Square. The two Koreas are still formally at war. Throughout the 1990s, it has for these reasons not been difficult to find politicians and commentators who believe that the antagonisms in east Asia are every bit as sharp and dangerous as they were in the 1980s. Nor do these people believe that the prospects of conflict have been greatly reduced by ASEAN or its Regional Forum. Meanwhile, China, North and South Korea, Taiwan and Vietnam continue to maintain large standing armies. Countries in south-east Asia are extending their navies (in Indonesia's case, with Habibie's decision simply to buy a large part of the fleet of the former German Democratic Republic). And although Japan's Self-Defence Forces still have fewer personnel than its Ministry of Posts and Telecommunications, that country's technical capacities for war now are formidable. Indeed, all that east Asia has seemed to lack are the secessionist nationalisms of south-eastern Europe and the former Soviet Union.

Yet the counter-arguments are at least as strong. The Chinese regime is not as precarious as some observers have wished to make it seem; indeed, the confirmation of the once unlikely Jiang Zemin's leadership by the party and by the President of the United States in 1997 makes it seem even less so. It is only liberal dogma, or forgetfulness, that prevents one seeing that a closed and relatively illiberal politics is perfectly compatible with a liberalizing economy. Studies of the local industries that contributed disproportionately to the growth of exports from China in the later 1980s and 1990s reveal that they have worked in relative harmony with public authorities, which do what they can to facilitate their success. The government's proposal in 1997 to liberalize its hitherto protected heavy industries, which has been followed by a series of measures to make the change financially easier, suggests that it is now driven more by economic interest than by the fear of abandoning through disemployment its last reliable bases of popular support. In conversation, younger civil servants in the economic ministries in Beijing are strikingly cool about the party, which they simply regard as an institution that has to maintain its national and international face. They accept that, when the leadership is more confident of its growing international power and no longer fears uncontrollable dissent, it will quietly transform itself into one of the inclusive ruling coalitions that have governed those states, Japan, for example, and South Korea (and, although Beijing would never admit it, perhaps Taiwan as well), that it takes as models. In North Korea, although the economy, unlike China's, is unsustainable, it seems possible that the present regime will continue in a more restrained form and pragmatically liberalize. Pyongyang will know that, in insisting that a precondition for talks on the reunification of the peninsula is that the United States withdraw its forces from the South, it is making sure they will not start. The South has anyway been frightened by the expense of the former West Germany's reunification with the East. If Kim Dae-jung were to pursue his plan for the coexistence and mutual recognition of two sovereign states and to persuade the leaders in Pyongyang to agree, the two Koreas will be free to benefit from their complementarity.

In principle, the issue of the formal independence of Taiwan still arouses anger in China. China did fire missiles into the Taiwan Strait to warn against campaigns for independence in the presidential election in 1996, and the new provisions of the Mutual Security Treaty between

Japan and the United States do for the first time commit the signatories to joint action on those issues, like conflict in the Taiwan Strait, that affect them both. In practice, however, the financial connections between China and Taiwan are so strong that China, which has the initiative, is as likely as not to learn from its accommodation of Hong Kong, and Japan and the United States could prudently discover that Taiwan is not an issue that affects them. To those who argue that China is bent on reasserting its former domination in the region, and will not acknowledge that its security lies in co-operating with others, the answer can be that it has never, unlike Japan, been an expansionist power, and that it can have no conceivable interest in direct confrontation. Its need and its growing power give it the incentive and the strength to bargain for economic concessions that other states can only dream of. The real fear would be of what the government in Beijing might do if it found itself unable to control opposition inside the country. But, so far at least, there is no clear sign of any region wishing, as some have predicted, to break away. Although there is an increasing number of unemployed and, from an economic point of view, excessive migration to the cities from the countryside, social disturbance, of which there is also little sign, would almost certainly not find a political voice. And there are few intellectuals in China, even in the newly cosmopolitan Shanghai, who believe that a competitive democracy yet makes sense for the country.

The counter-arguments would not be strong, of course, if states in the region were actively exercised by each other's internal politics. But they are not. Japan prudently observes the Western conventions. It did not join the other Asian states in refusing to sign the declaration after the first United Nations conference on human rights in Vienna in 1993, and it subsequently declared that it would regard gross violations of such rights as a reason to withhold its Overseas Development Assistance. Wisely, however, it did not suspend its yen loans after the confrontation in Tiananmen Square, and was the first subsequently to resume trade with China. It was the first also to resume aid to Burma/Myanmar after 1990. There had been talk in Japan itself in the early 1990s of facing up to what resentful American Congressmen regard as the responsibilities commensurate with economic power. Its main protagonist, Ichiro Ozawa, a former secretary general of the Liberal Democratic Party, has since failed in his attempt to turn his breakaway New Frontier Party into an electorally significant opposition, and Hashimoto has calmly taken as much as he thinks is wise of his case. Meanwhile, ASEAN has resisted criticism from the West and extended membership to Burma/Myanmar, thereby offsetting the assistance which, in return for privileges for its military intelligence, China has been giving the government there. Hashimoto and the members of ASEAN clearly believe that the best hope for peaceably practical connections between the states in east Asia lies in not taking a public position on each other's internal politics. The new China has everything to gain from doing the same.

VII

It is the international economy, not, in the classical sense of the term, international security that now matters. The effects of having to open national economies have in the past twenty years everywhere challenged what had come to seem a natural affinity between the practical and imaginative projects of the nation state. Practically, a government could be committed to the management of its own economy with capital controls, a self-determined fiscal policy and other such devices. Imaginatively, it could create the national community on which it could then depend by demonstrating this commitment and using it to extend welfare. Now, macroeconomic discretion is constrained and the political nation is losing one of its foundations. Alert Europeans have seen that the solution, difficult though it may be to pursue, lies in conceding sovereignty to a defensive monetary union. Asian politicians, by contrast, have barely begun to consider such a possibility.

It is commonly assumed that they do not need to. The solution to their present difficulties, commentators in the United States and the financial press insist, is to deregulate production, prices and the trade in goods and services and to re-regulate the financial sector. These measures naturally appeal to those abroad with the power to take advantage of them and to the institutions charged with exercising that power. But there is also an argument. The east Asian economies have practised what in Germany a century ago was called *Nationalökonomie*, and, as it was for Germany then, this has been a great success. Now, in the stronger economies as well as the weak, it is ceasing so obviously to be so. Some of the state enterprises, notably in Singapore, work better than many in the region that are private; others, in China for instance, Indonesia and the ex-socialist countries in the south-east, have been sustained for non-economic reasons, and do not. In all the east Asian economies, the banks have many non-performing loans and are still lax, assets are often not made the best of, firms hesitate to invest and consumers are cautious. In all but Japan, South Korea, Taiwan and Singapore, there is also a large and relatively poor population beyond the choked and sprawling cities.

Yet in all these national economies there has also been a political purpose. It is this that is more difficult to change. There are vested interests. The proposal to increase the powers of the Bank of Japan and the Ministry of Finance in Tokyo, for instance, is resisted by powerful interests elsewhere in the bureaucracy. It will pain Suharto to have to abandon the Chinese businessmen to whom he has given such lucrative monopolies, the national car project that he had given to one of his sons to direct, and Habibie's aviation industry. Politicians in Thailand and Malaysia will not find it easy to abandon compliant banks. More importantly, the political classes in east Asia remain convinced that control of the national economy and of citizens too is what their power consists in. Ito Hirobumi took the project from Prussia and adapted it for Japan. Later generations in Japan and elsewhere in east Asia adapted it to the circumstances of the Cold War and the formal demands of democracy. In Japan, the democracy has been constitutionally liberal, and since 1993 has shown signs of becoming more truly so. Elsewhere, it is either stalled, as in Thailand, by corruption and unresolved conflict, or suppressed, as in Indonesia, Malaysia, Singapore, South Korea and Taiwan, behind a façade of competition and 'Asian values', or still denied, as in China, by a single party.

Seen from the United States, such politics are instances of the end of democracy's prehistory. Seen from Britain, they are in their more orderly manifestations, like Singapore, the end of its own history: a model of how in the present international economy, where only the details of domestic policy can be disputed, one can have prosperity with order. But such views tell one more about the hopes of liberals in America and of a certain sort of post-socialist (and post-Conservative) in Britain than they do about east Asia itself. The countries there are now in an international history, subject to common constraints and an increasingly common schedule of desire. But they are also in their own histories. These are less ideological than ours, but no less fractious. They are more pragmatic, but have more open futures. Internationally, the states of east Asia will have little choice into the first decades of the next century but to observe the rules of security set by the United States, accept the vicissitudes of international finance, and profit as they can from Japan's power. Internally, they will have more political discretion. The question for these states later in the next century, as for those elsewhere, will be whether China acquires the power that the United States has had in this to set the terms for others.

Further Reading

There are comprehensive introductions to the recent past in *The Cambridge History of Japan*, vol. 6, edited by Peter Duus (Cambridge: Cambridge University Press, 1988), *The Cambridge History of China*, vol. 15, edited by Roderick McFarquhar and John K. Fairbank, (Cambridge: Cambridge University Press, 1987), and *The Cambridge History of Southeast Asia*, vol. 2, edited by Nicholas Tarling (Cambridge: Cambridge University Press, 1993). Bruce Cumings, *Korea's Place in the Sun: A Modern History* (New York: Norton, 1997) is a critical piece of writing by the foremost Western student of the Koreas since 1945. There are numerous accounts of Japan's recent economic history; none captures the spirit in the story as well as Shigeto Tsuru, *Japan's Capitalism: Creative Defeat and Beyond* (Cambridge: Cambridge University Press, 1993). Chalmers Johnson has been one of the most vigorous students of modern Japan in the West; his thoughts over the years are captured in the essays in *Japan: Who Governs? The Rise of the Developmental State* (New York: Norton, 1995). Four lectures by Ezra Vogel, *The Four Little Dragons: The Spread of Industrialisation in East Asia* (Cambridge MA: Harvard University Press, 1991), provide a clear introduction to Taiwan, South Korea, Singapore and Hong Kong. Robert Wade, *Governing the Market: Economic Theory and the Role of Government in East Asian Industrialisation* (Princeton: Princeton University Press, 1990) explains in detail how Taiwan and South Korea have achieved their growth. Hal

Hill, *The Indonesian Economy since 1966: Southeast Asia's Emerging Giant* (Cambridge: Cambridge University Press, 1996) is a full but more orthodox and technical account of its subject. The paper by Mitchell Bernard and John Ravenhill, 'Beyond Product Cycles and Flying Geese: Regionalisation, Hierarchy, and the Industrialisation of East Asia', *World Politics* (1995): 171–209, reviews the dispute about Japan's powers in the region. Walter Hatch and Kozo Yamamura's *Asia in Japan's Embrace: Building a Regional Production Alliance* (Cambridge: Cambridge University Press, 1996) is vividly first-hand. *Network Power: Japan and Asia*, edited by Peter J. Katzenstein and Takashi Shiraishi (Ithaca NY: Cornell University Press, 1997) is a collection of generally excellent essays on all aspects of Japan's relations with the rest of east Asia in the 1990s. Paul Krugman's article, 'The Myth of Asia's Miracle', *Foreign Affairs* 73, no. 6 (1994): 62–78, is in part a reply to a much publicized study from the World Bank the year before. The essays in *Confucian Traditions in East Asian Modernity: Moral Education and Economic Culture in Japan and the Four Mini-Dragons*, edited by Wei-ming Tu (Cambridge MA: Harvard University Press, 1996) are interesting and often conflicting appraisals of the nature and significance of this elusive subject. S. N. Eisenstadt, *Japanese Civilisation: A Comparative View* (Chicago: University of Chicago Press, 1996) is magisterial. John Dower's essays in *Japan in War and Peace: Essays on History, Race and Culture* (London: HarperCollins, 1995) are compelling readings of Japan during and after the Second World War. An article by John Boyd, British ambassador in Tokyo in the early 90s, on 'Opposition in Japan', *Government and Opposition* 32 (1997): 631–46, gives a wider sense of the political and economic predicaments in the country than its title might suggest. David

Martin Jones, *Political Development in Pacific Asia* (Cambridge: Polity Press, 1997) is particularly good on the politics of the south-east Asian states; the essays in *The Politics of Elections in Southeast Asia*, edited by Robert H. Taylor (Cambridge: Woodrow Wilson Center Press and Cambridge University Press, 1996) are also illuminating. No one has written more sensitively on the modern history of relations between Japan, the United States and China than Akira Iriye in *Across the Pacific: An Inner History of American–East Asian Relations* (Cambridge MA: Harvard University Press, 1967) and *China and Japan in the Global Setting* (Cambridge MA: Harvard University Press, 1992). Gerald Curtis, ed., *The United States, Japan, and Asia* (New York: The American Assembly, 1994) is an authoritative collection of papers. The *Financial Times* has the best reports on east Asia in the British press.